OLIVE

A Biographical Memoir of Olive Vergilia Blackmore

Patricia Blackmore Farrier

Copyright © 2024 by Patricia Blackmore Farrier

All rights reserved.

No portion of this publication may be copied, reproduced, stored in a retrieval system, or transmitted in any form or by any electronic or mechanical means whatsoever (including photocopying, electronic recording, or otherwise) without the prior written permission of the publisher.

2024 Pakaraima Publishing House

www.PakaraimaPublishingHouse.com

Hardcover ISBN: 979-8-9906760-0-8
Paperback ISBN: 979-8-9906760-1-5
E-Book ISBN: 979-8-9906760-2-2
Audiobook ISBN: 979-8-9906760-3-9

First Edition 2024

It is with immense gratitude that I dedicate this book to my
beloved family, who have been a constant source of
inspiration and support.

I cannot thank you enough for enriching my life
with your love and kindness.

PREFACE

Imagining an older person, especially someone over 70, as a trusting young child can be challenging. It's also difficult to picture an elderly person navigating the complexities of the modern world without occasionally being deceived. However, there are cases where old age and a sharp mind go hand in hand, proving that a long and rich life often brings the precious gifts of wisdom and sharp insight. The well-known maxim states, "It's not the years in your life, but the life in your years."

My mother, Mrs. Olive 'Dolly' Blackmore, lived a remarkable life. Born in 1911 and passing away at the age of 105 in 2016, she showed incredible strength in the face of life's challenges. Her achievements left a lasting impact on everyone who knew her, especially our family. Over the years, she became the matriarch of the Blackmore family in South Cummingsburg, Georgetown, Guyana. This was the culmination of a journey that spanned a long and remarkable life marked by consistent productivity and a phenomenal dedication to our well-being. My mother was both disciplined and compassionate, ensuring our family thrived in a loving home with stability and plenty of laughter—a testament to her wonderful personality.

She bore ten children during her life. Unfortunately, tragedy marked the early and late ends of this spectrum: the firstborn, Diane, passed away shortly before her first birthday, while the youngest, Lancelot, departed at the tender age of two. However, the remaining eight offspring matured into adulthood; as I pen this memoir, they are successful and enjoying their own later years. Even the youngest among us, Mervin, is comfortably in his seventies.

We have thrived, raising our own families and gaining our own wisdom throughout the years. And yet all who had the privilege of knowing my mother, Olive Blackmore, including her eight surviving children, regard her as a peerless mother, a matriarch par excellence. Without exaggeration, I firmly believe that she is among the finest people that British Guiana/Guyana has witnessed. The story of her maternal fortitude and achievements will unfold in the pages of this memoir, which strives to give my mother's life and accomplishments the recognition they deserve. I am pleased and excited to document Mom's story, hoping it brings enlightenment to my siblings, their offspring, and the dear friends and relatives of the Blackmore family.

Table of Contents

CHAPTER 1

RESILIENCE AMIDST TURMOIL

The remarkable woman who became Olive Blackmore was born as Olive Vergilia Joseph on May 23, 1911, in the captivating city of Georgetown, the heart of colonial Demerara in British Guiana. From the moment she arrived home from the hospital, her older brothers affectionately called her "Dolly," thrilled that their mother had brought home a baby doll. Friends and family continued to call her "Dolly" throughout her life. She was born into an exciting time of change—just a year after the first radio broadcast took place and one year before the sinking of the Titanic.

Georgetown, often hailed as the 'Garden City of the Caribbean,' was then a picturesque port city nestled in the northeastern coastal plains of South America. Towering trees, adorned with whitewashed bases, lined the streets in orderly grids. Canals, bordered by lush green grass, demarcated the thoroughfares. The streets were filled with stilted white wooden houses, crowned with vibrant red or green tin roofs and spacious windows shaded with Demerara shutters. A rainbow of fragrant flowers and fruit-bearing trees surrounded each home, and birds hopped from branch to branch, singing sweet melodies. Even the weather was pleasant; temperate trade winds coming in from the Atlantic provided relief from the tropical heat and humidity that were common elsewhere in the country.

Olive spent her formative years at 33 Howes Street in the vibrant Charlestown neighborhood. Guided and protected in the embrace of her parents, Edwin Hubert and Alice Joseph (née Jones), along with her elder brothers, Weston and Eric, and her younger sister Olga, Olive experienced a largely serene and joyful early childhood. Alice, Olive's mother, remains shrouded in a measure of mystery due to her untimely passing shortly after giving birth to Olga. But her influence on Olive's life lasted a lifetime.

In 1914, most of the world was dealing with the onset of the First World War, but Georgetown stayed mostly unaffected by the global upheaval. British Guiana was not directly involved in the war, but the colony contributed to the effort by providing raw materials and recruiting soldiers to serve in the British military. The nation did not entirely escape the troubles of the time, however. In 1918, when Olive was seven years old, the Spanish Flu pandemic brought fear and uncertainty to the people of Demerara, as it did throughout the world. The disease swept through Georgetown, causing illness and death, and left its destructive mark on the community, adding an extra layer of worry to their daily lives. Despite desperate attempts to control the disease's spread, quarantine measures and public health campaigns only partially mitigated its impact.

Despite these challenges, the Joseph family stayed strong and resilient, facing these difficult times together. As time passed, however, Edwin increasingly felt the weight of Alice's absence. Though he could care for his sons, Weston and Eric, he recognized his limitations in providing the appropriate care for his young daughters. Faced with this reality and the ongoing dangers posed by the pandemic, he made the difficult decision to entrust his motherless daughters to the care of his sister and her husband, who lived on the island of Barbados. Olive and Olga, at just seven and five, respectively, started a bittersweet sea journey from their home in Demerara to Barbados, saying goodbye to all the familiar faces and places that they knew. In Barbados, the young sisters found themselves dealing with the challenges of adjusting to a new place and beginning a new chapter of their lives, guided by their aunt and uncle.

Olive and Olga spent nine years on the island of Barbados, often called the "Land of the Flying Fish and Cou-Cou." Fortunately, much of their stay was one of contentment. Their father, Edwin, was a man of means; he was a skilled shipwright, landlord, and money lender. These enterprises earned him an above-average income. As such, he was able to provide financial support from afar. This ensured that Olive and Olga enjoyed a stable and comfortable existence in Barbados, even in the absence of their father's daily presence. The sisters were home-schooled by their aunt, who was very kind to them. Their aunt taught them important subjects and the social graces suitable for their status; thanks to the money Edwin provided for music tuition, they also became accomplished pianists.

However, the idyllic narrative eventually took an unsettling turn. Once they reached their teens and were old enough to understand more about their situation, the sisters discovered a disappointing truth: their aunt's husband was diverting some of the funds Edwin was sending for his own alcohol habit. Their uncle drank heavily, resulting in a lack of nutritious meals and other essential provisions for them. Olive, being resourceful, secretly wrote a letter about what she had discovered and gave it to a person she trusted who was traveling back to British Guiana. As soon as her father learned of the situation, he immediately arranged to have his daughters return to British Guiana.

Unfortunately, returning home led them from one challenge to another. The family situation had changed while they were away. During the girls' absence, their father, Edwin, had remarried, taking Etheline Taylor, a Barbadian neighbor, as his new wife. Sadly, their stepmother treated them poorly, making them endure hard work and denying them the care they desperately needed. Their father's attempts to help were unsuccessful, and his influence in his own home diminished. Edwin was distraught when Etheline refused to give food to his sons, so he decided to share his food with the two young men. Meanwhile, she created an atmosphere of fear and insisted that the girls, now 16 and 14, complete an excessive number of chores. Olive often recounted these challenging times in her later years.

Within this difficult atmosphere, Olive and Olga found solace in their elder brothers, Weston and Eric. Weston, who aspired to be a pharmacist, and Eric, who worked as a tally clerk at Sprostons and a tailor, offered unwavering support. Yet, their own struggles with

Etheline added to the household tension. Etheline's demands for Weston's financial contribution conflicted with Edwin's desire for Weston to bolster savings for his future. Despite Edwin's significant financial contributions to the family's well-being, Etheline's unrealistic expectations strained relationships. During this ongoing tense atmosphere, Edwin became ill with an unexplained malady, and his health worsened over time, making him even more vulnerable to Etheline's demands. Medical treatments did not work, and he eventually passed away, leaving his children orphaned.

After their father's death, Weston attempted to assert his legal claim over the family home and other properties within the home compound that belonged to his father, seeking to secure the inheritance for himself and his younger siblings. However, Etheline resisted. She strongly objected, insisting on her exclusive right to the inheritance. She even threatened Weston for pursuing his inheritance, warning him, "On the day of the court hearing, you will be a dead man."

More tragedy followed when Weston himself became seriously ill from a mysterious ailment. Sadly, he too passed away, leaving the Joseph siblings without their eldest brother and guardian. Weston died before the hearing, leaving Etheline's possession of the estate unchallenged.

After losing his brother, Eric sank into a state of depression and he began to lose his hair due to the stress of the situation. At that time, he became incapable of providing protection to his sisters. Olive and Olga, yearning for a sense of security, sought refuge with relatives, shifting between various households and enduring a life of hardship, moving 'from pillar to post'.

Weary of being unsettled and having no permanent place to live, Olive, with determination, secured employment at a garment factory, where she honed her skills in shirt-making. Once she was gainfully employed, she achieved financial independence and was able to support herself and her younger sister, Olga.

As the turbulent events of their early years settled, Olive reached a pivotal moment in her life, marking a significant turning point for herself and her sister, Olga. Her resilience and new job brought the sisters a sense of hope, lighting their path towards a brighter future. Despite the difficulties they knew they would encounter; their strong bond helped them navigate the uncertainties ahead. Olive and Olga built for themselves a sense of stability as they bravely confronted the unknown together.

CHAPTER 2

A LOVE STORY UNFOLDS

Olive's life changed forever when she met Bertrand McDonald Blackmore at her cousin's home. Affectionately known as Bertie, Bertrand was a lone twin, with his sibling passing shortly after birth. Bertie also had a half-brother, Joseph "Joe" Adolphus Blackmoore, and a half-sister, Ethel Irene Anthony (née Blackmore). When they first met, Bertie was already a widower, just six years older than Olive. However, fate had other plans, and the two fell deeply in love. The story of Bertie and Olive was about to begin—a love story that would endure for decades and build an amazing foundation for the generations that followed.

After a few months of getting to know each other, Olive and Bertie's friendship blossomed into a romantic relationship, and they officially became a couple. Olive dreamed of a future with Bertie, longing for a lifelong partnership. Their love for each other flourished, and they decided to share not just dreams and aspirations but also a home and life together. They settled into a peaceful neighborhood in

Georgetown, renting a house on Oronoque Street, Queenstown. It was a warm and inviting place to be, thanks to Olive's dedicated care and Bertie's penchant for cleanliness.

Their growing love led to the birth of their first child, Diane. Bertie's heart brimmed with joy as he wholeheartedly embraced the new role of fatherhood. Their home became a haven, where Bertie eagerly returned each evening with open arms, expressing his deep devotion to his daughter. Unfortunately, amid their joy, tragedy struck. As Diane started teething, she cried incessantly, so Bertie sought advice from a local pharmacist. The pharmacist prescribed medication that was too strong for the delicate child, tragically ending Diane's life before her first birthday. Grief overwhelmed Bertie; it took months for him to find solace, forgiveness, and healing.

Although Diane's passing cast a deep shadow on Olive and Bertie, it would not dim the bright future ahead for them or their family. As the sadness of her loss gradually faded with time, their love continued to deepen and took its formal beginning in the sanctity of their wedding, symbolizing their shared commitment and the blessing of their families. With the support of Bertie's mother, Margaret Theresa Dempster, fondly known as "TT," elaborate wedding preparations unfolded. TT not only assisted, but also helped pay for Olive's wedding gown and the subsequent reception. The devoted couple solemnly exchanged vows within the sacred walls of a Roman Catholic church, a testament to Bertie's unwavering faith and active participation in the Blessed Sacrament Guild. Olive, who had been born into the Anglican church, embraced Bertie's faith and converted to Roman Catholicism at his request.

The newlyweds began their married life together, filled with hope and shared dreams. It was an idyllic time for them. Bertie returned home from work each evening, greeted by the aroma of Olive's delicious, home-cooked meals and the embrace of his loving and growing family. With the addition of four children—two boys and two girls—Olive and Bertie began envisioning a future in a home of their own. Bertie, a man of action, purchased a plot of land at 341 Cummings Street, South Cummingsburg, and drafted the plans for a two-bedroom cottage. This was a pivotal moment for the Blackmore family. They were going to build a new life for themselves, in more ways than one.

Working as a carpenter and painter at the British Guiana Transport and Harbours Department (T&HD), Bertie brought his talents home. With the help of his kind neighbor, Mr. Correia, he built his new house in the evenings after work. They carefully built a sturdy cottage, elevated on ten-foot-tall stilts and distinguished by the inscription "TEETS" above the front door, in loving tribute to his mother, TT. The home, built with all the skill and love that Bertie had to offer, became the enduring cornerstone of the Blackmore family's life for generations to come.

Nestled among existing trees, Bertie's green thumb led to the cultivation of even more foliage at the Blackmores' new residence. The compound flourished with a variety of fruit trees, including breadfruit, mango, golden apple, cherry, soursop, dung, and guava. Bertie also constructed a fowl pen to accommodate the increasing number of chickens he reared. Over the years, thanks to his resourcefulness, the family was able to enjoy fresh eggs and sumptuous chicken-based meals ever so often.

In their charming new house, Olive's homemaking skills shone, revealing her versatility in various tasks. Her craftsmanship was evident in almost everything in the house. She decorated living spaces with beautiful handmade curtains, updating them regularly for a fresh feel. She was also a gifted cook, turning any available ingredients into delicious meals. In addition to their homegrown produce, Olive frequented the local market multiple times a week to buy fresh ingredients. Her positive rapport with vendors often led to receiving extra items as a gesture of appreciation.

Seeing how much Olive loved baking, Bertie built a special oven under their house to please her. Olive used this new installation a lot, especially on Wednesdays and Saturdays when she made delicious bread. She occasionally baked cakes, coconut buns, cassava pone, and conkies.

Olive and Bertie bore nine more children after Diane: Cedric Joseph, Patricia "Patsy" Bernadette, Mae "Marie" Olivia, Lawrence "Lorenzo" Bertrand, Francis Gordon "Gordon", Peter Mortimer "Monty", Claire Ann, Mervin Patrick, and Lancelot. Except for Lancelot, who was born at the nearby Georgetown Public Hospital, the rest of the children were born within the comforting walls of their home with a midwife's assistance. As Olive prepared for each new baby's arrival, Bertie took on the responsibility of caring for the other children, ensuring a smooth transition in their family dynamics. He brought them to the nearby home of his half-sister, Ethel Anthony, ensuring their well-being during this time. Continuing to do his part, Bertie used his carpentry skills to craft a wooden pram for his wife, which allowed her to easily take the infants and younger children to the nearby beautiful Promenade Gardens, a few blocks away.

Olive and Bertie created a warm and loving environment for their children. Through the ups and downs of parenthood, their unbreakable bond remained steadfast over the years, guiding them through life's challenges. As the Blackmores thrived, Olive and Bertie built a legacy of love that became a cherished cornerstone of their family for generations.

CHAPTER 3

A HAPPY FAMILY

Bertie and Olive, as protective parents, always balanced firmness with affection. Their parenting style, rooted in love, was somewhat stricter than what would be considered standard today. Bertie implemented a rule that when he returned from work, he wanted to find the children playing exclusively within the confines of their own yard. This meant that we could not wander into neighbors' yards, stand at the gate, or linger on the streets. He made it clear that he would not tolerate unnecessary conflicts with his neighbors. Bertie's intent was to protect his children from bullying or exploitation. He believed the family was large enough for the children to find companionship within. Later in life, we adopted this approach when raising our own children.

With plenty of experience as a seamstress, Olive applied her expertise to make clothing for her husband and children. With meticulous care, she ensured that Bertie and all nine Blackmore children were always well-dressed, particularly for important occasions like attending church. Moreover, in a manner reminiscent of her father, Olive took on the role of the household's financial steward. Bertie had a good job, but their family was large, and they needed to manage their finances wisely. She diligently saved coins in a small piggy bank can, building a reserve for unforeseen circumstances or special needs that might arise on a rainy day. Nonetheless, she was a generous soul, especially towards those who sought assistance at her doorstep, particularly those in need. Her compassionate and giving nature became a hallmark of her character; she exuded discipline, kindness, and generosity.

Each morning, it was customary for every child to greet both parents with a cheerful "Good morning!" The family also followed the tradition of saying grace before meals. Bertie maintained a strict stance on personal hygiene, emphasizing the importance of washing hands both before and after meals. The children were also required to hold hands while walking to and from school on busy streets. Before retiring for the night, the entire family gathered to recite the rosary, a ritual that Bertie, as family patriarch, led every evening. Then each child would say goodnight to both parents before turning in.

Bertie had two essential expectations for his children: to read and to be kind. These values were paramount to him, ensuring that the children were not only well-read but also displayed kindness in our interactions with others. He encouraged us to read books and use the dictionary to expand our vocabulary. Bertie, himself an avid reader, enjoyed publications such as Reader's Digest and other intriguing journals. Once, when Bertie's friends came over, he asked Marie to showcase her reading skills by reading aloud from the Reader's Digest. She proudly complied. This left Marie with a fond and lasting memory of her father.

Bertie kept a substantial medical reference book at home, a trusted resource that he consulted whenever any of the children became ill. This extensive medical guide, affectionately referred to by the family as the 'doctor book,' served as a constant "on-call" doctor in the household. Bertie would diligently hunt through its pages, seeking to understand the significance of the symptoms. It seems likely that this meticulous approach to medical matters stemmed from Diane's tragic death after Bertie received misguided advice from a local pharmacist. With the 'doctor book', Bertie made sure that he had a reliable backup medical resource for any future problems.

The Blackmores enjoyed socializing and hosted parties every New Year's Eve. The family frequently danced together to swing music playing on the radio. Bertie's love of music showed in his talented playing of the clarinet, banjo, and guitar, bringing joy to Olive and the family in the evenings. He played regularly during visits by his two best friends, who accompanied him on other instruments in raucous harmony. Their favorite song to perform was 'Sweet Sue, Just You.'

Like most families in British Guiana and many countries worldwide, Christmas was one of the most joyful seasons for the Blackmores. We dedicated the weeks leading up to the holiday to giving the house a face-lift, both inside and out, for the festive occasion. Each year, Bertie took charge of repainting parts of the house with the assistance of his sons. Together, they varnished the furniture and floors until everything gleamed. Olive, demonstrating her ingenuity and commitment to tradition, decorated the house with self-made red curtains and cultivated lush plants for display both indoors and outdoors. Guianese tradition and culture heavily influenced these preparations.

Olive's cooking skills shone even more brightly during the holiday season. In the days leading up to Christmas, she made many delicacies from scratch and even brewed homemade beverages. She prepared the deep-red sorrel drink, spicy ginger beer, and robust jamoon wine, storing the latter two in large jars. She also skillfully prepared cured ham, garlic pork, and the traditional Guianese black cake, incorporating specially dried fruits that underwent cleaning, washing, and sun-drying.

The family enjoyed the traditional Guianese Christmas breakfast of freshly baked bread dipped into the savory and spicy pepperpot stew. For dinner, Olive took immense pleasure in crafting a feast for her family featuring a delectable array of stewed, roasted, or baked chicken. The sight and aroma of her delicious dishes on the Christmas table were enough to tantalize the taste buds of everyone in the house. The children savored every morsel, to the quiet delight of Bertie and Olive. We were a family of modest means, but no one enjoyed a Christmas feast more than we did, proving that one does not need wealth to enjoy the most delicious meals. Among the festive treats provided for the children were apples and grapes, imported from North America by local merchants. During their transportation from North America, packing them in ice earned them the name "ice apples." To enhance the festive spirit, Bertie thoughtfully installed a candy machine under the house, ensuring the children had a delightful Christmas filled with sweet memories.

Every year, Bertie took the children window-shopping in downtown Georgetown, the main commercial area. We gleefully immersed ourselves in the sights and sounds of the festive season, reveling in the Christmas music and marvelous store decorations. During colonial times, despite Georgetown's tropical climate, decorations often included cotton wool, symbolizing snow.

Of course, Christmas is also a time for giving. Bertie Blackmore was like a real-life Father Christmas for his wife and children, using his talents to make special wooden Christmas gifts. One memorable year, he made a Morris chair, an early version of a reclining chair, for Olive to unwind at the end of each day. Another year, he created a large, white, wooden rocking horse for the children to enjoy. And in yet another clever creation, Bertie crafted a small wooden car with pedals for the boys to ride around in, giving them lots of fun. These gifts were particularly special because Bertie made them, putting his time and love into the presents. But while Bertie's craftsmanship in making gifts was impeccable, his venture into purchasing presents sometimes proved less successful.

One year, Bertie fulfilled my Christmas wish by buying me a sleep-and-wake doll, only to discover that it was defective—its eyes, instead of opening and closing as they should, were permanently closed. Seeing my disappointment on Christmas Day, Bertie ingeniously painted over the closed eyes, creating open ones and eliciting uproarious laughter from the entire family. Despite these occasional missteps, Christmas morning remained a source of joy for all the children. The experiences of those childhood Christmases, filled with homemade and creatively modified gifts, have endured as cherished memories for all of us. Together, all these efforts formed the heart of the Blackmore family's Christmas celebrations, rich in tradition, flavor, and happy memories.

As the years passed, Olive and Bertie's home became a sanctuary of love and faith. It wasn't just a house; it was home, a special place that has left a joyful, indelible mark on our hearts. It was a place where we learned lessons, made memories, and shared lots of laughter. Thanks to Bertie's strong leadership and Olive's caring nature, our home was a shining example of resilience, kindness, and unwavering commitment to family.

CHAPTER 4

BELOVED 'TT'

Margaret Theresa Dempster, who was affectionately known as 'TT' to her loved ones, was born on November 30, 1886. From a young age, TT's graceful demeanor captivated those around her, complemented by a voice that could soothe souls and a smile that warmed hearts. Her journey began in British Guiana with her parents, John and Margaret Dempster (née De Cambra). TT's only child, Bertie, held a special place in her heart.

Around the years 1929–1930, TT, then in her mid-forties, traveled to the beautiful island of Bermuda, joining her son Bertie, who had relocated there following the passing of his first wife. During this period, Bermuda faced significant challenges as it grappled with the worldwide economic hardships of the Great Depression. Across society, the downturn's effects led to social unrest and necessitated government intervention to support those most impacted by the crisis. The Great Depression hit Bermuda's economy particularly hard, leading to widespread unemployment, poverty, and financial instability that the country could not afford. The island's economy, heavily reliant on tourism and international trade, suffered greatly because of decreased visitor numbers and declining trade activity.

Setting up shop, TT engaged in dressmaking and established a storefront for West Indian produce. It was a challenging business at first, but her mastery as a seamstress earned her widespread recognition and popularity within the Bermuda community.

In Bermuda, TT eventually crossed paths with John James Caesar, a farmer and entrepreneur hailing from St. Kitts. A recent widower and father of nine children, John James, or "JJ," as he was known, was a prominent figure with the distinction of owning the first complete grocery store and meat market in Somerset, Bermuda. One day, when JJ was looking for West Indian provisions, fate brought them together. Mary, a friend, suggested TT's store. Their initial meeting was serendipitous, with a basket of 'rosy cheek' mangoes acting as the catalyst. A casual compliment referencing TT's own 'rosy cheeks' led to a genuine connection, one that deepened with time. TT's compassion shone through as she reached out to JJ's daughter, Irene, offering to teach her sewing skills, helping her to cope with the recent loss of her mother.

TT and JJ's union led to marriage just six months later, despite Irene's initial hesitation due to the pace of events. Their blended families bore testament to TT's compassion and JJ's resilience, a love story that spanned time and life's challenges.

TT and her son, Bertie, shared a strong bond. Bertie's love for his mother was deep, which he demonstrated not just in words but also in his actions. He was a strong protector, standing as a shield against any threat or disrespect toward TT. With TT's newfound security, Bertie returned to British Guiana, a decision that led him to meet Olive, changing the course of his life forever.

Olive found TT to be a reliable source of financial support, in contrast to others of the older generation who had been less than honorable in financial affairs. TT's husband's successful business in Bermuda allowed her to provide generous financial help to Bertie and his family in British Guiana. She regularly sent boxes by boat filled with fashionable clothing and non-perishable food items, bridging the gap between Bermuda and their home in British Guiana and helping Bertie and Olive provide for their family.

TT's generosity transcended borders, prompting her to visit Bertie and Olive in British Guiana with her step-granddaughter, Venita "Nita" Caesar. They had only intended to stay for a month, but the unexpected start of World War II significantly extended their plans. Their 'brief trip' extended to nearly twenty months, allowing them to forge enduring bonds.

Of course, TT's benevolence extended to her community in Bermuda, and after following her husband to St. Kitts after his retirement, she continued to selflessly assist the less fortunate. In December 1949, at the age of 63, TT's health finally faltered, marking the end of her remarkable journey and leaving a profound void in the hearts of those touched by her kindness. The multitudes lining the roads during her funeral procession demonstrated the heartfelt outpouring of respect that met her passing.

TT's life was filled with kindness, compassion, and a strong dedication to helping others. Her legacy of service and love continued to inspire generations, leaving a lasting impact on her family and the communities she served. TT's example—the love and support she gave her daughter-in-law over the years—provided her with a supportive parental figure that she hadn't had in years. For generations, TT's legacy of kindness and generosity lived on through Olive and the rest of the family.

CHAPTER 5

TRAGIC LOSSES

I n the year 1954, a cloud of sorrow and grief descended upon the Blackmore family. Bertie worked tirelessly at the T&HD, using every penny he earned to ensure his family's well-being. He spared no expense to ensure their happiness and comfort. But TT's death hit him hard. He struggled to bear the weight of his mother's loss, a deep wound that refused to heal even four years after her death. Additionally, the family's finances faced a new strain as TT's generosity ceased with her passing. Bertie had planned to rebuild the house to accommodate his large family, with financial help from TT. However, her death abruptly halted these renovation plans, leaving Bertie with a significant setback.

Bertie's coping mechanisms took a tragic turn as he grappled with his grief and the increased financial strain. His struggles with smoking and drinking, a means to numb the pain and anxiety, fluctuated from light to heavy, taking a toll on his health that exceeded the ability of the 'doctor book' to fix. He sought medical attention and received a diagnosis of hypertension. Then, a deafening noise from a passing plane startled him while he was at home, triggering a severe stroke that worsened his already fragile health. We rushed him to Georgetown Public Hospital in grave condition. Bertie's prognosis was not good; he was placed in the section of a ward usually reserved for the terminally ill.

Realizing that his days were almost over, Bertie yearned to spend his final hours in the comfort of his home. His children surrounded him with love and support as he slipped away, fulfilling his request. Cedric, Marie, Lawrence, Gordon, and I all bore witness to his passing. The cause of death, recorded as 'cerebral hemorrhage/hypertension' on his death certificate, was the somber culmination of his health struggles and the traumatic events leading up to his passing. The Blackmore household was shrouded in sorrow, marking not only a day of sadness but also the end of a significant chapter for the family.

Olive was not at home when Bertie passed away. She had gone to pick up his belongings from the T&HD. When she returned home, she was not surprised to hear the sad news; she had physically felt the moment of his passing.

Over the years, up until shortly before she herself passed away, the joyful memory of their last dance together to the song 'The Tennessee Waltz' came flooding back to her whenever she heard it playing on the radio. It always brought tears to her eyes, as well as a smile to her lips. She remained in love with Bertie until the day she died.

Bertie's wake was a gathering of loved ones held in the embrace of the Blackmores' home. Relatives, friends, and fellow members of the Blessed Sacrament Guild attended the funeral at the Cathedral of the Immaculate Conception. His final resting place was Le Repentir Cemetery. Olive was distraught by his loss. During this difficult time of mourning, she found solace in the support of relatives and friends.

But difficult days remained for the family. On November 1, 1954, just nine months after Bertie's death, there was another tragic and devastating blow. Olive, widowed at the early age of 42 with nine young children to care for, lost her youngest child, Lancelot.

Lancelot was an adorable child. He and Mervin, who were the youngest, often got into mischief. Whenever their older siblings bothered them, he would warn them, saying, "Ah gon tell Cedric!" Tragically, two-year-old Lancelot developed pneumonia and required hospitalization at Georgetown Public Hospital. I accompanied Mom there and cuddled him. Sadly, while waiting for the doctor to attend to him, he quietly passed away in my arms. Olive became gaunt from grief; she cried even more for her child, Lancelot, than she did for Bertie. She eventually found joy again in her life, but the impact of these deaths stayed with her. She lamented many times since then: "God gave me ten, and He took back two."

The Sacred Heart Roman Catholic Church on Main Street in Georgetown hosted Lancelot's funeral. All Saints' Day, November 1, marked his death, and All Souls Day, November 2, marked his burial. At the end of the funeral service, the parish priest, Father Kearney, SJ, observed Olive's sobbing and heartbreak. A close and friendly neighbor of the Marshall family who was at the funeral, told the priest that Olive had also just lost her husband a few months before. He immediately asked for her home address and visited her the following day. Understanding that the Blackmores had lost both a father and a child within less than a year, he took care to go over details regarding the family's financial and other needs. He then arranged for the St. Vincent de Paul Society, a renowned Catholic humanitarian organization, to provide assistance.

Father Kearney was a compassionate figure who became akin to a second "father" to the grieving family, offering Olive valuable assistance in various aspects of her life. He not only helped her with business matters, but he also facilitated support from different organizations. For example, as the Christmas season approached, marking Olive and her children's first holiday without Bertie, Father Kearney orchestrated a heartwarming surprise for the family. A few days before Christmas Eve, he arranged for several young women to bring the family an abundance of goodies. Later, a group of ladies from the Ladies of Charity organization delivered Christmas hampers. These thoughtful and generous gestures coordinated by Father Kearney added a touch of warmth and kindness to what would have otherwise been a challenging holiday season. The family deeply felt the blessing of having this kindly priest by their side.

Regrettably, while Bertie was an excellent provider in life, he passed away without having executed a will for his land and property. As a result, Olive found herself engaged in a prolonged legal process over his estate, shuttling to and from lawyers for nine long years to resolve the matter. Eventually, a trusted family friend, Ms. Dublin, recommended a lawyer who, with unwavering diligence, efficiently navigated the complexities of the legal system and allowed Olive to finally inherit his estate.

Olive struggled with both the loss of her husband and the financial difficulties that followed Bertie's death. But she found comfort in the love of her family and friends. Father Kearney and the community's support were a much-needed beacon of hope and warmth during this tough time. Despite everything she had suffered that year, Olive was thankful for her blessings and the strong bond she shared with her children. Bertie and Lancelot's memories lived on in their hearts, giving them strength as they built new memories without them.

CHAPTER 6

HEADS HELD HIGH

After Bertie and Lancelot passed away, Olive found herself faced with the immense responsibility of caring for eight young, fatherless children, marking a significant and lasting change in her life. In the immediate aftermath of Bertie's death, some well-intentioned relatives and friends suggested adoption or foster care for one or two of the children to lessen Olive's financial burden. Olive adamantly rejected these suggestions, declaring, "Not a bit of it!" Her own childhood separation from her father and brothers likely shaped this unwavering conviction. That experience had been difficult for her and Olga, and she was determined that her children would not suffer the same challenges. Olive remained resolute in ensuring that all her children remained together, living under one roof on Cummings Street.

Various individuals pressured Olive to sell her home. In one instance, a lawyer overstepped boundaries by proposing to Olive that she sell her home to generate funds for the family's upkeep.

Olive's response was swift, sharp, and filled with anger. She retorted, "If I sell my home, where would my children and I live?" Another neighbor extended an offer to purchase the property, further infuriating her. Olive again vehemently expressed her discontent, deeming their suggestions inconsiderate of her children's well-being. She had endured hardships during her late teenage years following her father's death, and she didn't want her children to experience the same. Despite these difficulties, she succeeded in keeping the home where she and Bertie had spent so much time and loved building together. In fact, not only was she able to remain following Bertie's death, but 341 Cummings Street became her permanent residence for the remainder of her very long life.

Her children helped, of course. Cedric, who was fourteen years old and the oldest of the siblings, played a crucial role in supporting his mother and siblings. He secured his initial employment at the T&HD as a 'tool room boy' for eight dollars a week. His function was simply to hand out tools to workers on request. His father, Bertie, had previously worked in the same department. While the work was helpful for the family, it was not the type of job that Cedric found attractive. He worked there for a short period, then found employment elsewhere.

During his early working years, Cedric established a unique approach to managing his salary. Rather than opening his pay packet himself, he would entrust it to his mother, Olive, to do so. Olive, in turn, allocated the money, always prioritizing the family's most essential needs. Impressed with Cedric's selflessness and generosity, she expressed her pride in him and encouraged him to set aside a portion for himself. His desires were modest; however, on occasion, he used his portion of the funds to purchase a movie ticket in the pit section of the cinema. Olive was incredibly proud of him and praised Cedric's admirable qualities many times over the years until her passing.

To supplement her limited financial income, Olive washed clothes for a woman in Georgetown. But Cedric intervened when he realized how unsanitary some of the clothes were, deciding it was not a suitable job for his mother. Without Olive's knowledge, Cedric informed the woman that his mother was no longer interested in washing clothes—a revelation that Olive discovered some time later.

As a widow raising eight youngsters, Olive made particularly sure that her children behaved with dignity and respect. Despite facing difficulties, she worked hard to give them the best care possible. She always reminded her children of her main rule: "Hold your head high and smile." She also often said, "Show me your company, and I'll tell you who you are," teaching them the importance of surrounding themselves with good people. The children followed her advice, choosing to spend time with decent and law-abiding members of the community. The siblings walked together to and from church every Sunday morning and actively participated in Sunday school and various children's clubs. With a love for singing, Lawrence and Gordon joined the choir, where they learned to sing not only in English but also in Latin. They both sang as sopranos in the choir at the Cathedral of the Immaculate Conception on Brickdam—a connection that endured as they remained staunch Catholics. Monty, on the other hand, sang with the choir at Sacred Heart Church.

Cedric utilized his diverse skills and talents to assist his family. He gave his brothers and friends haircuts, fixed broken domestic equipment, and attended to other issues around the house. But it wasn't all work and chores; the siblings also produced concerts at home and performed the hits of the day. Cedric sang Nat King Cole songs and played the harmonica, while the other boys used combs and foil as makeshift instruments. Monty and Mervin acted as clowns, and the girls sang daytime hits such as 'Struggle and Strife'.

Olive's routine included a visit to Bourda Market, conveniently located just a few short blocks from her residence. She bought fresh meat, fish, ground provisions, greens, and other fresh food items. However, financial constraints occasionally led to instances where her basket was not fully stocked. This predicament caused some embarrassment, as certain nosy neighbors openly scrutinized her purchases upon her return from the market. Due to this open judgment by neighbors, Olive initially began to stuff the bottom of her basket with objects to make it appear fuller. However, over time, she chose to disregard their intrusiveness and insensitive behavior. She maintained her dignity, knowing that she was doing everything possible for her family.

The family no longer enjoyed lavish meals as when Bertie was alive. Many times, they had to share very limited food among the eight children and Olive. However, they didn't feel poor when comparing themselves to their friends. They saw that they lived in a well-kept home that their mother owned and were well-dressed due to the beautiful clothes she made for them. They were also socially active in their church and community and happy due to the positive attitudes and laughter within their home.

Bertie's half-sister, Ethel, and her husband, Lemuel Fitzarnon Anthony, affectionately known as "Papa," and their two daughters, Enid Waveney Agard (née Anthony) and Cecily Yvonne McDonald (née Anthony), along with their families, as well as Lucille Barrow (née Parks), all displayed immense kindness and unwavering support to the Blackmore family after Bertrand's passing. Their generosity was immensely beneficial and deeply appreciated. Another close relative of Olive, Iris Jones, fondly referred to as Cousin Iris by the younger members of the family, also showed exceptional kindness and love towards the family. Olive's brother, Eric, made frequent visits to see her. He was quiet, laughed a lot, and liked to play crossword puzzles in the newspaper. He was also a talented tap dancer who brought moments of joy to her heart. The Marshalls and other good friends visited frequently as well. They could not replace Bertie in her life, but they helped Olive remember that she was part of a broader community of family and friends who loved her.

Olive became a member of the Sodality of the Blessed Virgin Mary, a Roman Catholic Marian society that convened once a week. This affiliation allowed her to engage with other Catholic women on a regular basis. She eagerly anticipated these gatherings as a source of companionship and support. Still attractive in her mid-forties, Olive, despite having eight children, drew the attention of some eligible bachelors who sought to fill the void left by her late husband, Bertie. However, for these gentlemen, their mission proved futile. Olive harbored no interest whatsoever in welcoming another partner into her life, whether for love or financial security. While it was not easy for her, Olive was determined to give her all to her eight growing children's proper upbringing. She made the suitors aware that her primary concern and sole focus remained on raising them and providing them with a good education. And she was not alone in this endeavor, because her children, particularly Cedric, the eldest, acted as vigilant guardians against potential suitors. They were steadfast in preventing anyone from taking Bertie's place. They positioned themselves as a protective barrier between their mother and any man attempting to be more than platonic in their approach, like the robust British Guiana sea defense. Cedric held deep affection for his mother and was fiercely protective of her, along with his three sisters, Patsy, Marie, and Claire.

The Blackmores, like most practicing Catholics in Guyana at the time, participated in the pre-dawn Christmas Novena, a special series of Holy Masses marking the nine days leading up to Christmas. Every morning from December 15 to December 23, they would rise early to attend the Novena Mass at Brickdam Cathedral. Monty, in keeping with the tradition of crafting items started by his father, made a nativity scene for the home every year. Lawrence and Gordon joined friends from the choir to sing carols on Christmas Eve. On Christmas Eve night, the whole family attended Midnight Mass, ushering in the holiday at the stroke of midnight—a joyous conclusion to a long day. In her later years, Olive often recounted, "The children were out of bed by five o'clock. They would get up, bathe, and so on, and then we would walk down to church. Trust the Lord, and He will see you through. I have so much to thank my loving Heavenly Father for... the discipline!" This reflection highlighted Olive's enduring faith and gratitude for the spiritual guidance that shaped her family's life throughout their time together.

Olive faced numerous challenges after Bertie's death, but she confronted them with unwavering resolve and determination, relying on her faith in God to keep her family united. The household remained filled with happiness, often resonating with laughter, music, and dancing. Despite facing tough times, she taught everyone under her roof that some of the most precious parts of family life were priceless.

CHAPTER 7

EDUCATION IS THE KEY

Olive's strength and her children's unity helped the Black-more family not just get by but even thrive despite tough times. During this phase of her life, Olive witnessed the positive development of her children in both education and work. Her commitment to their education remained unwavering. She knew that education would be the key to their later success and independence, and she was determined to ensure that they received the best education possible. All the children initially attended the well-regarded Teacher Marshall Kindergarten School. Upon completion, they progressed to Queenstown Roman Catholic Primary School, under the leadership of the nationally renowned educator, Percival Francis Loncke. Olive's children took different paths from there, however. Monty transferred to Bedford Methodist on Bourda Street. Gordon attended Chatham High School, where he showcased his academic prowess. Claire, on the other hand, pursued her education at St. Joseph's Commercial School, where she became proficient in Gregg shorthand writing.

My siblings pursued their studies rigorously. Cedric had to drop out of high school, and I could not begin high school because we needed to seek employment shortly after our father's death to support our younger brothers and sisters—a sacrifice we both gladly made. At the age of 55, I successfully earned my high school diploma in the United States with honors, fulfilling a long-delayed life goal. My husband and children were extremely proud of my persistence and admired my determination.

When we were younger, my siblings were my priority. One Christmas, despite our limited finances, I was able to purchase a special gift for my siblings: the popular and exciting Ludo game. Witnessing their enthusiasm as they eagerly began playing brought me immense joy. While the gift may not have been extravagant, it achieved its intended purpose, ensuring my brothers and sisters had a happy Christmas.

Olive's dedication to preparing her children to succeed in the world paid off. Over time, all of us found well-paying jobs. After working as a tool boy at T&HD, Cedric secured employment as a reporter for the Daily Argosy newspaper, then at the Guyana Marketing Corporation as a payroll supervisor, and finally as an assistant accountant. Subsequently, he emigrated to the United States, where he held various positions. He worked for the City of New York's Department of Homeless Services for 35 years, retiring as a superintendent. His success was largely due to his policy of treating the homeless with dignity.

As for myself, thanks to the guidance of my cousin, Cecily McDonald, a commercial teacher who prepared me for my professional career, I was able to leverage my proficiency in Pitman's shorthand, typewriting, and advanced English. During my career, I attained various significant secretarial roles. I am truly grateful for those opportunities, as they allowed me to provide financial assistance to the family during difficult times. I began my professional journey as an assistant clerk for a small company earning four dollars per week. Subsequently, I transitioned to the Guyana Geological Survey, where I served as a switchboard operator/typist for four years. After that, I worked at the Deeds Registry before transferring to the Public and Police Service Commissions, where I initially held the position of a typist clerk. Later, for ten years, I served as a confidential secretary to the Secretary of the Commission. Afterward, I joined the United Nations Action Program for Economic Co-operation (UNAPEC). Later, in England, I worked as a secretary at two different companies to support my own family. After returning from London, I worked as a confidential secretary to the general manager at the Guyana Marketing Corporation until I emigrated to the United States to join my children. My husband, Francis, joined us later.

Marie began her professional career as a secretary at a private office. She later served as a personal secretary in several government departments, even undertaking the responsibility of typing speeches for the president of Guyana. She also contributed her expertise as secretary to the general manager at the Rice Board. Marie's commitment to her career led to her successfully completing short courses in English and Political Science at the University of Guyana. After emigrating to the United States, she seamlessly transitioned to a position as a home health aide, a job that she embraced until retirement. She was always in high demand as a home health aide because she had a unique ability to care for even the most difficult patients. They even awarded her "Home Health Aide of the Year" three times and held a celebratory party in her honor.

Lawrence, aka Lorenzo, began his career as a recording engineer at the Government Information Service, where he recorded speeches by senior government officials and worked on the Ministry of Education's radio program Broadcast for Schools. Later, Lawrence was a producer of several musical programs on the Guyana Broadcasting Service, such as *GBS Roundabout, Back to Work, Sounds Caribbean,* and *Rolling Home.* With his vast knowledge of music across various genres and his unique musical preferences, which included artists such as Hugh Masakela, Ray Conniff, and James Last—names previously unknown in Guyana—Lawrence quickly gained widespread popularity among Guyanese radio listeners. His unconventional selection of music transcended the norm, captivating not only the attention and admiration of Olive and his siblings but also turning them into some of his most devoted fans. Even the country's Prime Minister, Forbes Burnham, listened regularly to his radio programs. In one particularly humorous encounter with the PM, the PM teasingly called Lawrence "drainpipe," referring to his excessively stylish trousers. Lawrence countered by asking the PM, "What about those socks?" A few hours later, after the PM had returned from lunch, Lorenzo noticed that the PM had changed his socks. Lawrence eventually emigrated to Canada, where he held various roles, including that of record press engineer, until his retirement.

Gordon commenced his professional journey with a three-year tenure at the Transport and Harbours Department (T&HD),

where his father had worked. Following this, he joined the Ministry of Education, where he worked in various senior positions, which allowed him to make substantial financial contributions to the household over the years and to successfully pursue a Bachelor of Social Science degree in Economics and Business Administration at the University of Guyana. He then worked on a hydropower project at the Upper Mazaruni Development Authority. Having accepted a Government of Guyana scholarship, he ventured to England, accompanied by his wife, Desiree, to pursue postgraduate studies in International Marketing Management - an achievement that brought Olive immense joy. After returning to Guyana, Gordon worked in various managerial and executive positions at the Guyana Fisheries Corporation and the Ministry of Trade and Industry. Sometime later, he emigrated to New York, where he worked in various positions, including in the investment banking division at the Union Bank of Switzerland prior to his retirement.

During early adulthood, Monty was a trained juggler, performing at various concerts. He and a group of close friends formed the musical band 'The Jets,' which rapidly gained popularity. Monty showcased remarkable musical talent, excelling on the guitar, keyboard, drums, and mandolin. His musical acumen was most likely inherited from Bertie. Their lively rehearsals, held at home, provided delightful entertainment for Olive. Subsequently, Monty expanded his artistic pursuits into theater. He enrolled in a three-year course at the Croydon College of Design and Technology in England, delving into the intricacies of stage lighting design. While Olive celebrated his professional growth abroad, she deeply missed him during his prolonged absence. After Monty returned to

Guyana from England, the National Culture Center in Georgetown appointed him as production manager and lighting director. It was at this venue that Monty held his first event as an executive producer - a stage adaptation of "The Sound of Music." Over a decade later, after Monty had immigrated to the United States, he wrote and directed "Parade of Nations," a production depicting the coming of Christ, which featured a cast of over two hundred people with live animals and was presented to an audience of over six thousand.

Upon graduating from St. Joseph's Commercial School in Georgetown, Claire found employment at the Guyana Postal Service. She diligently served in various capacities within the institution, including accounting and balancing, which she thoroughly enjoyed. She steadily ascended through the ranks until her well-deserved retirement. After emigrating to the United States, she became a patient care coordinator and later a home health aide until her second retirement.

Mervin, the youngest of the siblings, demonstrated a natural aptitude for servicing and repairing vehicles of all kinds. He was also a jack-of-all-trades, helping Olive with carpentry and plumbing around the house. He spent three years in the army, during which time he worked primarily as a mechanic. This inherent talent led him to pursue formal training as a mechanic at the Guyana Industrial Training Center and the Guyana Technical Institute, a vocation that would become his lifelong passion and profession.

The successful and diverse careers of all her children brought Olive much joy and pride as she recognized that the sacrifices she and her husband, the father of her children, had made over the years bore good fruit, for which she constantly praised the Lord.

Olive, herself, contributed significantly to the home by employing her sewing skills. She continued her career as a seamstress, working from home. She created an array of garments, from working attire to special occasion outfits, not only for her children but also for others. Being self-employed brought her contentment and happiness, allowing her a great deal of independence and freedom for the remainder of her life.

Thanks to years of careful financial management, Olive made the most of her family's resources. A shrewd investor, Olive took advantage of the opportunity to build another house on her property using a loan from the New Building Society, which prided itself on providing soft loans to smaller property owners. This allowed her to earn extra income by renting out the additional property, contributing to the family's upward mobility. She even adorned the new house with the name "Olive" over the front door, a testament to her vision.

Now financially comfortable, Olive could effortlessly manage bills and undertake the upkeep and renovation of both houses on Cummings Street. Her pursuit of perfection and careful planning showcased her business acumen. She sought additional loans from the New Building Society to facilitate repairs or expansions required for the houses over the decades. One can vividly picture her engaging in discussions with the loan manager to articulate the purpose and necessity for each loan. Her persuasive skills and effectiveness ensured success with every loan application, showcasing her financial acumen. Demonstrating financial responsibility, Olive meticulously adhered to the repayment schedules for every loan.

The presence of good neighbors like the Marshalls and other cherished family friends, including Cousin Iris, Carrie Griffith, affectionately known as 'Sister Carrie,' and her three daughters, Eulene and her two sisters, always brought merriment to the household. Regular visits from Sister Lily, Ulric, Rita Barton, and steadfast friends like Mrs. Charlotte Bayley, Miss Vye, Miss Penera, Miss Dublin, and Mr. Russell, a good friend of Eric, enriched the family's social life. James Chan, a dear family friend and neighbor, along with his children, formed a special connection with the Blackmore siblings. Their visits were always delightful, and they held a deep affection for Olive. Additionally, Lorene Grant (née Blackmore), Lois Griffith (née Blackmore), Faith Harding (née Blackmore), Laurel Blackmore, Patrick Blackmore, and Evette Joseph were regular visitors to Olive over the years. Thanks in part to these family and friends, the Blackmore home was always a hub of warmth and camaraderie.

Olive found herself in a significantly improved position to maintain the standards she aspired to as both a mother and homemaker, with her children gainfully employed and contributing financially to the household. After struggling to deal with the aftermath of Bertie's passing, their combined incomes eventually propelled them back into the middle class, restoring the Blackmore family to its former position. Due to Olive's careful management of household finances and the support of her children, the family transitioned from a position of need to one of relative abundance, symbolizing the fruits of their collective labor.

CHAPTER 8

THE YEARS OF CELEBRATION

As they entered adulthood, the children attended celebrations, parties, and weddings. Among the brothers, hosting gatherings became a customary affair at their Cummings Street residence. Olive preferred these events over those held at other locations, choosing to closely monitor them with a watchful and nurturing eye instead of letting her children wander off elsewhere. She found it difficult to rest until each of her children returned safely home from their nights out.

The siblings had their own vibrant circle of friends, all of whom were equally outgoing. They loved singing and dancing together and shared lots of jokes and laughter. Albert Alstrom, Cedric Blackmore, and Terry Chase, close friends of the Blackmore family, organized the A-B-C Easter Monday Picnic, one of the major annual events. Very popular personalities of the day were regular attendees. The tradition continued for years but came to an end when most of the organizers emigrated. Olive's heart swelled with pride as she noticed the friends her young adult children had chosen. These friends consistently demonstrated respect for Olive and her home. Numerous times, she told her children happily, "You all have nice friends."

Then the dating era began, and Olive, with her skilled hands, crafted beautiful party dresses for her three daughters. Like Cedric, all the Blackmore brothers were extremely protective of their three sisters, ensuring none of their friends showed any disrespect. Olive established a firm curfew of 9:00 PM for visitors to leave, which she would enforce by the gradual closure of windows—a subtle cue signaling the end of the evening. The brothers' affection for their mother was evident in the way they always made time for her, such as when Cedric stayed with Olive every 'Old Year's Night' to welcome the New Year together. Subsequently, he would depart for a party with his friends.

Each of us eventually married, walking up the aisle as individuals and emerging as married couples. Olive's heart swelled with pride as she observed her children's chosen spouses, their bonds of respect mirroring the family values she instilled.

The first to tie the knot was Marie, who exchanged vows with Godwin Hilbert Smith at Our Lady of Fatima Catholic Church on August 27, 1966. Godwin was one of the country's top athletes. Marie's marriage eventually bore fruit with the arrival of two daughters, Michelle Ann Smith and Nicola Munika Smith.

The second union among the Blackmore siblings was my own marriage to Francis Quamina Farrier, a renowned dramatist and award-winning author in Guyana. Notably, he was the first author in the Caribbean to write a soap opera for radio in Guyana.

Our matrimonial ceremony took place at the Cathedral of the Immaculate Conception, Brickdam, Georgetown, on April 29, 1967. Lemuel Fitzarnon 'Papa' Anthony, the husband of my aunt, Ethel, walked me up the aisle. Unfortunately, my brother Monty was unable to attend our wedding because he had recently been involved in a motorcycle accident and was hospitalized. This marital alliance brought my two daughters, Arlene Zoisa Farrier and Venita Ayodele Farrier.

On September 26, 1970, Cedric entered matrimony with Claudette Eugenie Carrington, who served as the Secretary to the Fire Chief of the Guyana Fire Service. This union resulted in the birth of two children, Abina Adiola Blackmore and Cedric Alexander Blackmore, Jr. Tragically, Claudette passed away on December 1, 2007, at the age of 60.

Lawrence, the second son among the siblings, got married in October 1973 in Toronto, Canada, to Claire Marilyn Nichols, a former typist at the Office of the President in Guyana. Their marital union brought forth two children, Nicholas "Nicolas" Xavier Blackmore and Laurel Marietta Blackmore.

Claire, the youngest sister, exchanged vows with Jerome William Murray, a telephone technician, on December 1, 1973. The ceremony took place at the Sacred Heart Roman Catholic Church. From their union, two children, Jermaine Peter Murray and Lisa Ann Murray, were born.

Gordon, the third son, entered marital bliss with Desiree Anne Duncan on June 26, 1977. Desiree, a dedicated schoolteacher, impacted the lives of many students at the Trinity Methodist School in Georgetown over the course of several years. The couple, served as supportive uncle and aunt and played a vital role in assisting their nieces and nephews with their various educational endeavors over the years.

In Guyana, Monty, the fourth son, tied the knot for the first time with Leslyn Clarke, a trained dancer; their union blessed them with a son, Kevin Kwesi Blackmore. Some years later, he entered his second marriage to Daunne Cecelia Schultz, a former schoolteacher and renowned Guyanese singer. The couple welcomed two more children into their lives, Rawle Anthony Blackmore and Cheryl Ashley Blackmore.

Mervin, the youngest of the Blackmore siblings, married Deborah Christina Whyte, a secretary at a reputable firm. In 1977, a civil ceremony at the General Post Office in Georgetown formalized their union. Mervin Ian Blackmore, Jr., is the couple's only child.

Each of these weddings was an occasion for celebration and joy throughout the family, and in every case, except for Lawrence's ceremony (held in Toronto, Canada), Olive played an active and integral role behind the scenes, helping to meticulously prepare. In a marvelous demonstration of her creative prowess, Olive personally designed and crafted exquisite wedding gowns for all three of her daughters. Her artistic touch even extended to sewing dresses and outfits for her granddaughters.

In addition to her fashionable contributions, Olive generally took charge of baking the wedding cakes, although she delegated the intricate decorative icing to the expert hands of Mrs. Devonish, a trusted family friend. Olive's brother, Eric, maintained close connections with the family throughout, making frequent visits and participating in these joyous celebrations. Notably, he played a special and cherished role in escorting Marie and Claire up the aisle on their wedding days, as well as acting as father-of-the-groom to his nephews. Olive's nieces, nephews and extended family were all involved in the celebrations. Brenda Saul, Joy Mighty, Keith Agard, Carolanne Aaron, Junior Agard, Malcolm McDonald, Dawn McDonald and Juneann McDonald were especially close to Olive and the family over the years.

Olive consistently displayed a sense of fairness that extended to everyone under her figurative roof. Her sons and daughters-in-law truly felt just as loved and accepted as her own blood children. They all called her 'Moms' out of respect and affection. In the occasional instances where couples faced challenges with each other, Olive always refrained from taking sides, maintaining an impartial stance. Approachable and compassionate, she offered motherly advice, when necessary, to all parties involved. Additionally, she cherished the idea of married couples spending as much time together as possible. She knew that time spent together was irreplaceable—the foundation of any strong family, including her own.

CHAPTER 9

BELOVED GRANNY

Olive was affectionately known as 'Granny' by all her grandchildren and great-grandchildren. She was a no-nonsense grandmother, setting clear expectations and boundaries for her family. She demanded respect for elders and insisted on courteous expressions such as good morning, good afternoon, goodnight, please and thank you. She was a woman of unwavering discipline, using verbal admonishments or, when needed, a firm hand—methods deemed acceptable in that era. She did not tolerate rudeness or any form of swearing. She even frowned at anyone who said the word "damn." Despite her strict exterior, Olive exuded kindness, love, and care. Her goal was for her home to be a haven for her extended family where they felt a sense of security and to create joyful memories that she herself did not experience for many years of her youth. Approachable and empathetic, she served as a reliable confidante for anyone in need of explanations, advice on delicate issues, or just her stable presence.

Olive was a devoted grandmother who eagerly offered to babysit her grandchildren whenever needed, whether it was for a quick errand or an extended period, always showing unwavering support and care. Her generosity helped many of us achieve goals that would have been difficult without her. For example, in July 1969, Francis and I embarked on a journey to Banff, Alberta, Canada, where he participated in a summer course in theater and journalism at the Banff School of Fine Arts, University of Alberta. E.R. Braithwaite, the renowned Guyanese author of 'To Sir, with Love,' generously sponsored this. At the time, our daughter Arlene was just shy of a year old. We knew that traveling with her to Banff would be challenging. Despite my initial reluctance, we entrusted her to the loving care of Olive, who proved to be a wonderful grandmother. With the support of Olive, Arlene's loving relatives, and our elderly domestic helper, Ms. Iris, everything proceeded seamlessly during the six weeks that Francis and I were away. It was during this time that a deep bond took root between grandmother and granddaughter, a connection that lasted until Olive's passing years later. I stayed with my friend Carol Cunha in Toronto while Francis completed his course. It was a difficult time for me; I missed my little toddler dearly, even crying myself to sleep several nights.

Cummings Street served as the bustling epicenter for the Blackmore family, even after my siblings and I had grown and started homes of our own. It was a place where everyone gathered almost daily before dispersing to their respective homes for the night. Recognizing the need for more space to accommodate her growing family and shrewdly managing her finances, Olive made the thoughtful decision to transform the two-bedroom cottage that Bertie had built with such care into a more expansive three-bedroom house. She was very involved in their lives, seeing most of them almost every day. Michelle and Nicola lived with her during their childhood; Arlene and Venita lived in the neighboring house, and Abina lived further down Cummings Street. Later, Jermaine and Lisa also stayed with Olive, and Mervin Jr. spent time with her every weekday afternoon after school. We were fortunate that so many of our children had the opportunity to spend time with their grandmother.

Olive's grandchildren adored her, but they particularly cherished the enchanting moments when she told 'old-time stories.' Despite hearing them repeatedly, the tales remained captivating as Olive, endowed with an almost photographic memory, narrated each one with unwavering precision, almost as if she were reading them from a book. She had a remarkable mind for details; she could even recall prices down to the penny for items she had purchased many years earlier, adding a vivid and nostalgic touch to her storytelling. They sometimes complained to her about their place in the school line, saying it was because of their height. Olive, who was only 5 feet tall herself, scoffed, saying, "Y'all have good height!"

Olive enjoyed watching her grandchildren play. When the weather was sunny, she would often sit by a window and watch them play hopscotch, hide and seek, and other popular 1970s childhood games. When it rained, the children would venture indoors to play board games, jacks, or cards. Her love for music and dance from her youth, especially the waltz and foxtrot, did not prevent her from enjoying the current music of the day. She often challenged her grandchildren to compete against her dancing to popular soca music, her beaming smile lighting up the room as they all moved to the rhythm. Michelle, Arlene, Nicola, and Venita attended ballet and folk dance classes at the National School of Dance twice a week. Following their classes, they would return to her house for refreshments. In one notable performance to a large, sold-out live audience, the four girls showcased an African folk dance at the National Cultural Center, earning them a front-page feature in the top national newspaper the next day. Olive beamed with delight and pride at their achievement. The girls also attended weekly piano lessons nearby and practiced on the piano in Olive's living room on the days between lessons. They occasionally enjoyed hearing Olive herself play. Her house had always been filled with music, and thanks to her granddaughters, it remained so for years.

As her grandchildren entered preadolescence, Olive arranged a playhouse for them in the lower part of her house. Using their experience in ballet, folk dance, and piano, as well as their exposure to theater, primarily through my husband Francis, the grandchildren organized a variety show for their parents and their parents' work colleagues. The enterprising children even sold tickets for admission to their performance and cleverly included an intermission during which they offered refreshments made by Olive, showcasing their entrepreneurial spirit. With the proceeds, they indulged in treats like candy and fruit drinks. They were still young, after all!

Olive's home was a source of love and delicious food. The grand-children loved simple, quick-to-make snacks like 'egg and rice,' which Olive occasionally prepared for them. She would sit at her dining table with a large bowl of food, and the grandchildren would patiently line up, waiting for her to spoon-feed each of them. Little

Venita, brimming with boundless energy, ingeniously turned this dining experience to her advantage. She began a lively circuit after each bite, running through the house, down the back staircase, across the yard, and up the front staircase for another spoonful, repeating this delightful routine until she finished the meal.

Olive loved her home, but she also loved the countryside. On occasion, my husband, Francis, treated her and the grandchildren to leisurely drives along the picturesque East Coast and East Bank of Demerara. Along the way, they would make stops at quaint village shops and local markets. She relished the change of scenery, the lively conversations of her grandchildren, and the diverse musical tunes playing on the car radio in the background. On one occasion, Francis chartered a small plane and flew her and me to the Mazaruni region, a beautiful, forested, and remote area in Guyana. That was an experience that none of us will ever forget.

On many weekends, we attended movie nights at the Starlight Drive-in theater, situated along the lower East Coast of Demerara, overlooking the Atlantic Ocean. Olive, along with all her grandchildren, would pile into cars filled with a delectable spread of food and drinks that she had prepared for the occasion. On the journey along the seawall road leading to their destination, the grandchildren added to the merriment with songs and jokes. Upon arrival, anticipation filled the air as they eagerly scanned the crowd, hoping to spot school friends also relishing the cinematic experience. Even before the movie began, a magical atmosphere enveloped the cars in the lot amid laughter, play, and the invigorating ocean breeze.

Every Sunday, Mervin would take Olive to Mass at her regular church, Our Lady of Fatima. She never wanted to miss Sunday

Mass. Mervin also ensured that she attended national events, such as the vibrant Mashramani celebrations. Although she enjoyed the events, the pull of home and her advancing years generally meant that she quickly tired and often asked, "When are we going back home?" This was a routine, even during her attendance at beloved afternoon tea parties and events she cherished.

Each year, Olive played host to a gathering of elderly ladies, accompanied by a local priest, for an evening of rosary recitation. Following the prayers, the attendees indulged in her homemade treats and good conversation before parting ways. Olive upheld the tradition by insisting her grandchildren be present. Uncontrollable giggles from the youths often disrupted the solemnity of the event as they observed some of the guests' mannerisms. The infectious laughter often persisted despite Olive's sternest glances. To her dismay, these inappropriate, uncontrollable bouts of laughter also occurred during events such as the Christmas pageant at Sacred Heart Church and the Festival of Carols concert at Brickdam Cathedral, adding an unexpected and humorous element to these otherwise serious affairs.

My second daughter, Venita, was a warm and sensitive girl, though sometimes direct. Olive misunderstood her straightforwardness as rudeness, but it was just Venita being honest. Venita loved her grandmother and enjoyed watching Olive sew beautiful clothes on her old Singer sewing machine. Seeing this interest, Olive taught her how to handmake simple dresses for her dolls. As Venita grew up, she happily gave her grandmother haircuts and occasionally styled her hair. They were very close.

In 1978, I encouraged my husband, Francis, to pursue studies in performing arts and journalism at the University of Middlesex, England. It represented a big move for us, but I thought the opportunity was one that he could not pass up. In 1979, I resigned my position and accompanied him, along with our daughters, for four years abroad. Throughout this period, I continued working as a secretary at two large companies to help with the upkeep of the family.

It was difficult to be so far away from Olive for such a long time. Throughout the four years my family resided in England, we did our best to maintain regular contact with her. I sent photographs to keep her updated on Arlene and Venita's physical development as they transitioned from pre-teens to teenagers. Upon our return to Guyana, Francis was appointed Director of Drama in the Ministry of Culture. The girls gained admission to The Bishops' High School, one of the premier high schools in the country, joining their cousins, Michelle and Nicola.

Although she was proud of their academic accomplishments, Olive also encouraged her grandchildren to enjoy their teenage years and became an advocate for them whenever they begged their parents for permission to go to parties. She even made beautiful party dresses for them on short notice when asked. When she was young, she lived a very sheltered life and rarely had the opportunity to attend parties. She wanted her grandchildren to enjoy their youth and have happy memories.

Olive's grandchildren all successfully graduated high school and each of them secured lucrative and esteemed positions. Some of them pursued educational and career opportunities abroad. Olive, filled with happiness and gratitude, was a little sad to see her family spreading out across the world, but she continually thanked God for the numerous blessings that she had received. Having been widowed at the tender age of 42 and enduring the loss of two out of her ten children, she was overjoyed that her remaining eight children not only survived into adulthood but also flourished, leading successful lives and establishing their own families in Guyana and elsewhere. She often reflected on her life journey with pride, saying, "I gave birth to ten children, and God took back two—the first and the last." The remaining eight all grew up, got married, and achieved self-sufficiency, contributing to their communities, embodying her values of resilience and determination.

CHAPTER 10

SAFE TRAVELS

Then came the time when Olive embarked on several vacations abroad. Her house on Cummings Street no longer served as a hub for childcare, and her children had established their own homes and careers, freeing her up to explore the world. She first travelled to Canada, before visiting the United States. With children residing in both countries eagerly awaiting her arrival, Olive first stayed with her son Lawrence and his family in Canada. Upon arriving late-night in Toronto, she was amazed by the abundance of streetlights, a stark contrast to what she had seen in the now-independent Cooperative Republic of Guyana. Recalling her astonishment, she exclaimed, "If you see lights, ah tell ya! And the cars...by the millions, ah tell ya!" It was a remarkable experience for her. She spent a memorable year in Canada with them.

While living with Cedric in the United States, she happily took care of Abina and Cedric Jr. while their parents were at work. In New York, Olive started doing the morning exercises she saw on television. She would stretch and touch her toes, challenging others to try. She also went on a short vacation to Trinidad and Tobago. Through all her travels, she always stayed devoted to her home in Georgetown, arranging for its upkeep in her absence. Olive never went back to Barbados, however.

Olive not only enjoyed being a guest for others but also welcomed visitors from abroad. During one memorable occasion, her mother-in-law TT's stepdaughters, Martha and Christiana, along with step-granddaughter Venita "Nita," visited and stayed at her home. Their time together was filled with joy as they fondly reminisced about TT, sharing story after story from years ago.

My family and I also traveled a fair amount. Francis and I enjoyed a few days in Bermuda several months before the birth of our daughter, Venita Ayodele. Later, on our way to England, we returned there with our two young daughters. Years later, seeking some solitude and relaxation, I embarked again on a solo trip to beautiful Bermuda and spent a few weeks of quality time meeting with our stepcousins, which was enjoyable and relaxing. I seized the opportunity to explore Bermuda College as a potential educational institution for our daughter, Venita, who did eventually pursue her studies there. Consequently, Venita lived in Bermuda for her first two years of college.

During Olive's visit to New York City, Venita planned various activities to introduce her grandmother to the best of the city. Together, we attended several Broadway shows, including the timeless annual 'Christmas Spectacular' at the iconic Radio City Music Hall and the famous *Phantom of the Opera* musical, both of which Olive found thoroughly enjoyable. However, her expectations were sometimes amusing. After the *Phantom of the Opera* show, Olive remarked in a slightly disappointed tone, "It was nice, but I thought I would have seen Oprah!" Additionally, Venita orchestrated a Staten Island Ferry cruise across the Hudson River and a visit to the Statue of Liberty. She even exposed Olive to cosmic wonders by immersing her in the captivating virtual reality production of "The Big Bang" at the Hayden Planetarium, an experience that had no parallel in Guyana.

During her visits to New York, Arlene also went to great lengths to ensure her grandmother's comfort and joy. This entailed embarking on numerous extended drives to explore places of interest or visit relatives and friends residing at considerable distances. One such trip included a visit to see Cicely McDonald and her family, who had settled in Orange, New Jersey. Arlene vividly recalls Olive's reactions during nighttime drives, noting her continuous awe at the dazzling lights surrounding them. Amusingly, Olive would occasionally playfully fuss about the distance covered, exclaiming, "We might as well be driving to Guyana!" a mere 20 minutes into the journey; however, she never slept a wink during these rides despite complaining about their duration.

Olive traveled to several cities in the United States, including Washington, D.C., to visit friends and relatives. During her time in the nation's capital, she seized the opportunity to explore the outskirts of the White House, the official residence of the president. One notable visit coincided with Arlene's graduation from the University of the District of Columbia. As her feet hurt after walking to the venue in her fancy shoes, Olive boldly decided to remove them, proceeding to walk barefoot down the street, unconcerned about onlookers. Olive had always stressed the importance of education for all her children and grandchildren. Her heart swelled with pride and joy as she witnessed Arlene don the traditional graduation cap and gown, take the stage, and receive her well-earned degree, with honors no less.

Although Olive enjoyed the sights and experiences during her trips abroad, her heart yearned for the simple joys of spending quality time with her children, a desire that overshadowed all the external attractions. Despite the allure of foreign experiences, an internal conflict persisted within Olive. She enjoyed everything she saw and loved her children, but she longed to be back home in Guyana, surrounded by the children and grandchildren who resided there, with a special emphasis on her youngest child, Mervin, and her grandson, Jermaine.

The cold winters were one thing Olive didn't like about the countries she visited. She believed Guyanese people struggled in colder places and might 'crop out.' She felt strongly connected to her homeland, saying, "I prefer to die in my beautiful Guyana and meet my Savior, Jesus Christ, who blessed me with a comfortable and happy home for me and my family." When she visited New York, she sometimes asked me to go back home to Guyana to take care of the house, especially as she got older. I thought about this request many times, wanting to care for her.

As Olive got older and traveling became too much of a challenge for her, I took the chance to spend time with her when Francis visited Guyana for work. I stayed with her for three months, doing various things together, such as seeing friends and family, going to church on Sundays, and taking her to medical appointments. My brother, Mervin, kindly drove us around, and we enjoyed spending time with him and his family. Olive also received visits from my brother Lawrence in Toronto, as well as Gordon and Claire in Brooklyn. She really loved these visits. She knew that the days when we all lived close by were past, but it was nice to relive these days a bit during our visits, once again being surrounded by family in the home that had been the center of the Blackmore story for so many decades.

CHAPTER 11

THE GOLDEN YEARS

E ven in her golden years, Olive maintained a stoic and upright posture, holding her head high in a display of dignity and physical fitness remarkable for her age. She adamantly refused to use a walking cane, determined not to show any signs of aging or frailty. She was resolute in preserving her fitness and independence. For a while, she kept coloring her hair black, though eventually this transitioned into a shimmering silver crown on her head—a testament to the passage of time. Well into her centennial years, she continued to apply ruby-red lipstick, a vibrant expression of her vitality.

Her fitness and independence were likely due, in large part, to the fact that she adhered to a disciplined routine, beginning her day at 5:00 AM with the recitation of her rosary and a dedicated exercise regimen. She consistently began and ended her day with a comforting cup of something hot to drink—usually bush tea, such as lemongrass or hot cocoa. She ate sensibly; her preferred breakfast was a bowl of cream of wheat, a taste she acquired during a holiday in the United States. Occasionally, she would opt for Quaker oats or cornmeal porridge. Once a month, she would take a dose of bitters that she claimed cleansed her system.

Despite having a modest appetite, Olive spent a lot of time in the kitchen, crafting meals and an array of homemade fermented beverages from carambola, sourie, pineapple, and ginger. Always hospitable, she loved offering meals or glasses of her various concoctions to anyone visiting her home. By 12:00 noon each day, she had usually prepared lunch for the entire extended family and anyone else who might be around. Seeing her family and friends enjoy the meals and drinks she made always brought her much joy. She always advised people to arrive at her house with an appetite! Politely declining her offer of a meal was never an easy feat. Prominent among her meals were homemade bread, baked twice a week; on Saturdays, either a sizable sponge cake or coconut buns would also grace the table. Occasionally, she treated loved ones to custard blocks or ice cream. Her pepperpot was outstanding, and her split pea cook-up rice was consistently delicious. On Sundays, she often cooked metemgee, a traditional Guyanese dish with root vegetables, coconut cream, duff, and fish. Everyone frequently enjoyed her tasty chicken curry, chicken chowmein, saltfish cakes, and many other enticing dishes, ensuring her table was always filled with enthusiastic guests.

Gardening was one of Olive's favorite hobbies. This could sometimes be a bit risky where trees were concerned. Despite our family's apprehensions, she fearlessly climbed the banister of the outdoor stair landing on several occasions, using a long stick with a hook at the end to skillfully dislodge mangoes from the nearby tree. Equally daring, she stood on one of her windowsills and clutched onto a window frame for stability and used the same stick to reach for breadfruit from the towering breadfruit tree. This sight, simultaneously awe-inspiring and deeply concerning, showed Olive's determination. Beyond her treetop endeavors, she diligently swept the yard with a pointer broom and routinely burned organic trash.

Her days were active, but not her nights. Olive liked to wake up early, but she went to bed by 9:00 p.m. She did not like any noise or activity in her house after that time. No matter what anyone else was doing, she made sure to shut down everything by then. She would move plants outside, close windows, and turn off the television and lights. Those of us who were accustomed to later evenings sometimes found this a little vexing. However, the results were undeniable; remarkably, Olive's healthy lifestyle prevented her from ever needing hospitalization.

Olive stayed updated on the news by reading newspapers every day. She had strong opinions about current events and would readily share them with others. Usually, she verbally recounted the news in such detail that others had no need to read it themselves. Possessing a wealth of common sense and keen observation skills, she commented in detail on the evolving culture from the colonial era to the present. She expressed concern about the deteriorating standards in the country, including frequent problems with garbage collection and rising crime rates. Olive also expressed frustration about the difficulty in getting basic food items without the proper connections. She was concerned about safety, and she felt increasingly uneasy about wearing jewelry outside her home due to the fear of theft. Olive, who was always industrious herself, found laziness to be bothersome and disliked men who did not work. Despite these problems, she loved Guyana and preferred to stay in her home at Cummings Street even into her advanced age.

Over the years, Olive actively participated in Unity meetings in Guyana. Unity, a renowned non-profit organization rooted in the United States, provides practical and uplifting resources to help individuals of all faiths apply positive spiritual principles in their lives. Olive primarily gravitated towards the Unity branch in Guyana, yet she consistently attended meetings during her visits to the United States. She liked the positive and uplifting talks that delved into various religious principles. The core of Unity's teachings was accepting others' strengths, not judging, loving and forgiving, respecting yourself to earn respect, aiming to be your best self, believing in your abilities, giving support, and much more. The values it promotes align strongly with those Olive had believed in and practiced throughout her entire life. She also enjoyed reading books that discussed and espoused similar values. During my time residing in England, I utilized my work breaks to visit the library, where I sought out inspirational books by authors such as Catherine Ponder and other renowned writers. Over time, I gathered a collection of these books. I selected one of my favorites, "The Dynamic Laws of Healing," and sent it to Olive. Her response indicated that she thoroughly enjoyed the book.

Her dedication to unity was not just theoretical; she applied it to her own life as well. In her later years, Olive set aside a lifelong grievance and extended a warm welcome to her half-sister, Eunice Joseph. Eunice visited Olive on a few occasions, participating in two of her birthday celebrations, including her milestone 100th birthday. Unfortunately, Eunice, who had lost her sight earlier in life, has since passed away.

Mervin, Olive's youngest child, played a crucial role in her later years. He showed exceptional dedication and love as a son as she aged. Even when Olive was still able to move around easily, Mervin would drive her to Bourda Market and wait patiently to take her back home. He also made sure she got to church every Sunday. Mervin went out of his way to welcome any visiting relatives and friends at Timehri International Airport, even if they arrived late at night. He didn't mind the inconvenience and was always ready to make them feel comfortable. He also offered to take visitors on tours of the city and countryside, making sure they felt welcome and cared for during their stay.

Olive's children always made her birthdays special with organized celebrations. They threw a surprise party for her 80th birthday, which brought her a lot of joy. They also planned parties for major milestone birthdays, such as her 85th, 90th, 95th, and especially her remarkable 100th birthday. For her centennial celebration, preparations began months in advance, and many distinguished guests attended, including the Mayor of Georgetown. The festivities on her birthday included a morning Holy Mass at Our Lady of Fatima Church and an elaborate party with over fifty guests at Kirkpatrick's Restaurant and Gardens in Georgetown. Among the attendees were Bishop Francis Dean Alleyne, OSB, and Monsignor Terrence Montrose. The occasion was a particularly grand and memorable affair, with Olive, overjoyed, dancing with her eldest son, Cedric. Her large family, including children, grandchildren, and numerous close relatives, had gathered from far and wide to honor her on this momentous occasion; several flew into Guyana from abroad just to help Olive celebrate her remarkable century of life. It was a truly special celebration, which even earned her a feature in a prominent newspaper.

Olive had always been a mainstay of the community, but after reaching the impressive milestone of turning a hundred, she became even more of a local celebrity in her neighborhood. The policewomen from the nearby Alberttown police station, just two blocks away, made regular visits on occasions like Mother's Day, birthdays, and Christmas. They would bring gifts and spend a generous amount of time, at least half an hour, engaging in heartfelt conversations with her. Both Olive and the policewomen valued these visits immensely.

During this time, Joycelyn Loncke, a musical artist, invited Olive to attend a concert at Queen's College in Georgetown. The concert featured the renowned young band of the era, First Born, who delivered an immensely entertaining performance. The group directly acknowledged Olive, much to everyone's delight. They dedicated one of their songs to her, and after the rendition, a band member even left the stage, approached her in the audience, and affectionately kissed her forehead. After this, in a gesture of respect, he took her hands and gently kissed them before going down on his knees to reverently kiss both of her feet. The audience responded with enthusiastic and sustained applause, appreciating the heartfelt tribute to the remarkable centenarian. Olive, of course, was humbled and beaming with pleasure.

Nor did reaching this remarkable milestone slow her down. Well past her hundredth birthday, Olive remained active for years. During one of my visits to Guyana, when Olive was 103 years old, I organized a delightful afternoon for her with a group of elderly ladies. With Bernice Mansell and Deborah Blackmore's assistance, we gathered a bunch of lovely ladies from the Nazareth Home on Carmichael Street and the St. Vincent De Paul Senior Citizens Home in Georgetown. The purpose of this gathering was to create a special occasion for these elderly ladies to enjoy each other's company, with Olive graciously playing the role of their welcoming hostess, just as she had done for so many people over so many years in her home. The atmosphere was one of joy and camaraderie, and it is safe to say that everyone had a 'senior blast' at Olive's home. Just as she had done for more than seven decades, Olive made sure everyone felt welcomed, appreciated, and loved.

CHAPTER 12

TWILIGHT HAS COME

Even in the twilight of Olive's life, she continued to dwell in her home on Cummings Street. It was now part of a much larger enclave that had been built up and added to over the years. Her home, situated at the farthest end of the compound, held a special place in the family enclave. Even as her eyesight declined, Olive would often sit in one of her favorite chairs, looking out the window to the yard and street, as she always did. She was still sharp, but she began to feel the weight of her years, especially since she had outlived so many of the people who had been important in her life. She would often remark, "I am a forlorn bird! Weston gone, Eric gone, and Olga gone. All my friends are gone, and I am still here. Why doesn't the Lord come and take me? I'm ready to go to my long last home and be with my Bertie!"

Olive's social circle had by now dwindled. All her close friends who had once affectionately called her 'Dolly' had passed away, and they were just memories. Most of her children and grandchildren had scattered across distant lands, making their homes in the United States and Canada. Consequently, her home was not as vibrant with the presence of friends and relatives as it had been in the past. Increasingly, she hoped that her children living abroad would move back to Guyana. She believed they would have better lives with fresh food and no cold winters, leading to longer and healthier lives.

Michelle, Olive's eldest grandchild, first lived in the middle house but later moved to the front house of the compound, which Marie had bought. Michelle was always there for her grandmother, visiting her daily without fail. Michelle, who was a talented chef, often cooked homemade meals for Olive, bringing her joy with each delicious dish, especially as she was no longer able to cook as she once had. These visits were more than just about food; they were moments of genuine connection, filled with laughter, jokes, and heartfelt conversations. Driven by deep love for her grandmother, Michelle made sure Olive's later years were enjoyable. Olive cherished Michelle's lively sense of humor, finding comfort and happiness in their playful banter and shared jokes, which always lifted her spirits. She knew that she could not bring her entire extended family home, but she cherished the family that was there.

Over time, Olive's eyesight noticeably worsened. Concerned about her vision, we took her to see an eye doctor. The news was discouraging: Olive would probably lose her sight completely within a year. Unhappy with this diagnosis, we sought another opinion, and a different eye doctor suggested that a laser treatment could offer some hope. But Olive's children couldn't agree on whether she should have the surgery, which was risky considering her age. Although Olive herself was in favor of the operation, her family decided against it due to concerns about the risks. As a result, Olive's vision got even worse, and she became less mobile. Unfortunately, a few months later, it became clear that Olive's eyesight was indeed failing. Despite her initial hopes, her vision continued to deteriorate until she eventually became completely blind.

Even after losing her sight completely, Olive remained strong and cheerful, grateful to God for each day. Her family rallied around her, offering care and companionship. Her children, whether near or far, prioritized spending precious time with her, sharing stories and laughter. As her ability to do everyday tasks drastically declined, her children decided to hire home-care professionals to help. It began with nighttime caregivers, but soon full-time support was necessary to ensure Olive had assistance around the clock.

Despite facing physical challenges, Olive was determined to maintain her routine, even when arthritis started to bother her knees. Surprisingly, she never complained. In fact, when offered help, she usually firmly refused, saying, "I'm not an invalid! Leave me alone!" Her determination to stay independent remained strong despite the obstacles she faced. Even at the age of 105, Olive warmly welcomed visitors to her home, including the President of Guyana, David Arthur Granger. Although her hearing had also declined somewhat, she loved chatting with her guests and listening to the television and music. Jim Reeves was her favorite musician, and her caregivers frequently played his music for her to enjoy. Olive had hearing aids, but she didn't like using them much because she found them bothersome, despite her hearing impairment.

Olive found happiness and comfort in phone calls from her children living abroad. Of course, her home was always open to visits from her children, grandchildren, and friends, making it a warm and inviting place for family gatherings. Cecily, Dawn Hackett (née McDonald), Juneann Daniels (née McDonald), and Carolann Aaron (née Agard) consistently made it a priority to check in on Olive whenever they returned to Guyana. Additionally, Lorene Grant, Bertie's second cousin, would occasionally drop by for an afternoon chat, contributing to the warmth of Olive's social circle. Even my friend, Pamela Lloyd (née Carrington), her mother, and her sister, Philippa Perry (née Carrington), paid visits.

Throughout her long and joyful life, Olive held tightly to her Catholic faith, finding comfort in praying the rosary regularly. Despite facing increasing physical challenges, she remained devoted to her spirituality. A priest or a lay Eucharistic minister would bring Holy Communion to her home as part of her religious rituals. This was something she deeply valued and appreciated.

Olive had been Mervin's sole parental figure for most of his life, following the death of his father when he was very young. He visited her every day, sometimes even more than once, especially as she got older, and her sight failed. The family greatly appreciated Mervin's constant care and love for Olive during both her happy and difficult times. She knew how much Mervin cared for her, and she treasured him deeply for his endless love. Mervin shared a special bond with Olive. He was her closest companion in her final years, and the last of her children she was with before she passed away.

On August 23, 2016, Olive, our beloved family matriarch, passed away. Francis called our home in Maryland from Guyana to share the devastating news of my mother's passing, leaving us stunned and grief-stricken. He was the last family member to see her alive that day, having visited her for lunch a few hours earlier. She had greeted him when he arrived, but she was asleep when he left. Although it was heartbreaking to hear, I felt incredibly blessed that God allowed her to live such a rich and full life until the remarkable age of 105.

Olive's death certificate listed "cardiopulmonary arrest" as the cause of her passing. Our Lady of Fatima Catholic Church in Bourda, Georgetown, where she had often attended Mass, hosted her funeral. The gathering to remember and celebrate her life was deeply heartfelt and, unsurprisingly, well-attended. We referred to Monsignor Terrence Montrose as Fr. Monty. Monty led the service. Olive's grandson, Jermaine, put together a playlist with songs by Jim Reeves. Fr. Monty, Richard Van Sluytman, and I delivered the tributes. Unfortunately, my brother Lawrence couldn't make it from Toronto due to health reasons, but his daughter Laurel came to represent the family and read from the Scriptures. Mervin's son, Mervin Jr., gave a particularly moving eulogy, capturing the essence of her life. The Joseph family made a special contribution to support the funeral arrangements, showing their respect for Olive, their beloved matriarch.

After Olive passed away, her children started the process of executing her will. Mervin, who held the power of attorney, spearheaded the process. With the help of a lawyer, they sold Olive's houses and divided the money fairly among the children and grandchildren. Everyone worked together, and the whole process went quickly and smoothly. Olive did not want her children to go through the legal ordeal that she had experienced after the deaths of both her father, Edwin, and husband, Bertie, so she wisely ensured that all her affairs were in order well before her passing.

Olive's legacy lives on through her many descendants, who uphold the values she cherished. Her deep love for family, sense of duty, and respect for tradition continue to guide us and our children. Despite enduring the devastating loss of her husband and two children early in life, Olive found immense joy in witnessing her remaining eight children's remarkable accomplishments, watching proudly as they built their own families. They loved her deeply, and all of them provided both financial support and other forms of assistance over the years to ensure her well-being.

Olive's steadfast faith and resilience helped her overcome an enormous range of challenges. Whenever faced with difficulty, she would repeat the phrase "Divine order... divine order... divine order," always trusting that things would work out. Her children and grandchildren have inherited this mantra.

Olive's passing has left an irreplaceable void, once filled with her unwavering warmth and determination. Nevertheless, her life stands as an enduring testament to resilience, love, and her boundless devotion to both her family and faith. While her departure marked the end of an era, her memory continues to shine brightly within all of us as a beacon of strength and a testament to a life lived with purpose and grace.

Epilogue

As I bring this heartfelt memoir dedicated to Olive, my mother, mentor, and role model, to a close, I am acutely aware of the enduring impact she has had on my life.

Embracing the roles of wife and mother, I willingly provided support in various ways and gladly made sacrifices to contribute to the successes of my husband and children. Witnessing their numerous achievements and benevolent deeds, I am grateful to God for the role I played in their respective journeys.

The memory of my mom, Olive, occupies my thoughts daily. In conversations with my siblings, we fondly and joyfully recall her, cherishing the many beautiful memories we shared from her long and fruitful life.

~ REST IN ETERNAL PEACE DEAR MOM ~

Acknowledgments

As I bring this biographical memoir documenting the life of my beloved mother, Olive Vergilia Blackmore, to a close, I feel compelled to express my heartfelt gratitude to those who have provided invaluable assistance throughout this journey.

Foremost, my sincere thanks extend to Mrs. Philippa Carrington Perry, whose suggestion and encouragement prompted the inception of this memoir dedicated to my mother. Philippa offered her insight just weeks after my mom's passing in 2016. Subsequently, I discreetly collected information from my siblings and other relatives, aiming to make the published memoir a delightful surprise and cherished keepsake for them.

I am also grateful to Venita "Nita" Smith, the step-granddaughter of my grandmother, TT. Her unique contributions to this memoir, capturing TT's life during her time in Bermuda, add an important dimension to the story.

A special acknowledgement goes to my husband, Francis, whose assistance with some of the typing and editing proved invaluable. I also want to express my gratitude to my older daughter, Arlene, for providing the necessary tools, including a computer, as well as her invaluable competence in checking historical family records for valuable information. The meticulous proofreading and insightful suggestions for improvement came from my younger daughter, Venita, who also took charge of the overall publishing of the book.

Every individual mentioned has played an indispensable role in our family history, intricately weaving their contributions into the very fabric of this memoir. Their collective dedication and support have been essential in bringing this narrative to fruition, making the journey not only possible but also profoundly meaningful. Thank you, everyone.

APPENDIX 1

MY TRIBUTE AT OLIVE'S FUNERAL
ON BEHALF OF HER EIGHT CHILDREN

"Thank you Bishop Alleyne, Monsignor Montrose, Richard Van Sluytman, Gabriel Lall, and those faithful priests who took Holy Communion to my mom, Olive Blackmore, at 341 Cummings Street, every First Friday of the month, and on other occasions, after she became unable to attend Mass. We are now here to celebrate her Life, which took place at her home, on Tuesday August 23. My Mom Olive Blackmore has gone to be with the Lord after a long and blessed life, of 105 years. What a journey! What an achievement! I can say without reservation, that my mom was a devout Catholic. She prayed the rosary every day, and she tried never to miss Sunday Mass. We are eternally grateful that Mom was loved and respected by the priests, religious and parishioners at whichever parish she belonged - especially here at Our Lady of Fatima. My seven siblings and I were raised by both our dad - who has gone to be with the Lord many years - and our Mom, to be good Christians - kind, respectful, generous, honest and to see Christ in everyone; and to always be thankful for the blessing God has bestowed on us.

My Mom Olive Blackmore was a great mother. She sacrificed so much for her children, especially after we lost our dad. While we were so young. She was a very good seamstress who made beautiful clothing for us, including our wedding gowns, and clothes for my brothers when they were young. Mom was certainly all that a good mother should be. She was my mentor and role model, who taught me by words and deeds about being a good mother to my two daughters, Arlene and Venita, and a faithful and devoted wife to my husband, Francis. Thanks to my seven siblings, my supportive husband, my two daughters, my many nieces and nephews, relatives, and friends, for all the love and care they gave to the Family matriarch over the years.

I would like to give special thanks, and express my sincere gratitude to my youngest brother, Mervin, who is based here in Guyana, for all the love, care, and dedication which he showered on our mom, over the decades. Mervin went the extra mile over and over again, making so many sacrifices in caring for mom, as the rest of us were so far away, and I thank him from the bottom of my heart. I must also thank my niece, Michelle, Mom's oldest grandchild, for her continuous loving support of Mom over the years. Thanks to the dedicated caregivers who looked after Mom during her declining years. Also, the doctors who checked her health situation over the years. Thank you so much. We all thank you most sincerely for your dedicated service. I thank God for blessing our dear Mom with such a long and productive life. I particularly admired her for her faith in God, her strength, resilience, and her tenacity in keeping herself and Family together, especially in those tough and challenging years after her husband died and before her children began to work and brought much-needed income to contribute to the up-keep of the home. May her beautiful soul rest in eternal peace."

Appendix 2

Fr. Christian P. Huebner, Parochial Vicar, St Mary of the Mills Parish, Laurel, Maryland, USA, kindly wrote this Tribute for this Memoir of Olive Blackmore:

An ancient Christian custom refers to death as "falling asleep in the Lord". The great hope and consolation of a disciple of Jesus Christ, is the knowledge that He is Lord of the living and the dead, and that in Him, death has been overthrown. For those who are made one in the Body of Christ through baptism and faith, who eat his Flesh and drink his Blood in the Eucharist. Even if they should die, they will live. Falling asleep in the Lord means that we will rise again on the last day in the resurrection of the living.

Olive's pilgrimage in earthly life ended in her 105th year of a life well lived. In many ways, her end was as many would desire following a long and faithful life, rich in the blessings of family and bonds of love. In other ways, her end was not as many would choose: in God's Providence, she fell asleep in Christ without the presence of her children at her bedside. Francis, her son-in-law was present.

Father, thy will be done! This is the prayer of Our Lord, and of His disciples. He alone holds the ends of our lives in His divine wisdom, and we trust that He chooses our ends, with whatever blessing or agony they may hold, as a mysterious gift of His grace. Many of the Church's great saints throughout the ages have met their end in ways not desirable, through the eyes of the world, but in the light of faith we see - and they now see far more than us - that this was part of the mysterious plan of God's redemption of the world in Christ. Death is the last enemy; but because of Jesus Christ, it has been transformed into the way to eternal life. May our sister, Olive, rest in peace, beholding her Lord face to face, and awaiting the resurrection.

FR. JACK BERARD:

"The loveliest masterpiece of the heart of God
is the love of a Mother"
St Therese of Lisieux

REVEREND PASTOR MAE FLOYD:

"God has given to us a special gift - Our Mother
Joy to brighten our days and
Peace to fill our hearts."

Appendix 3

Weston Joseph

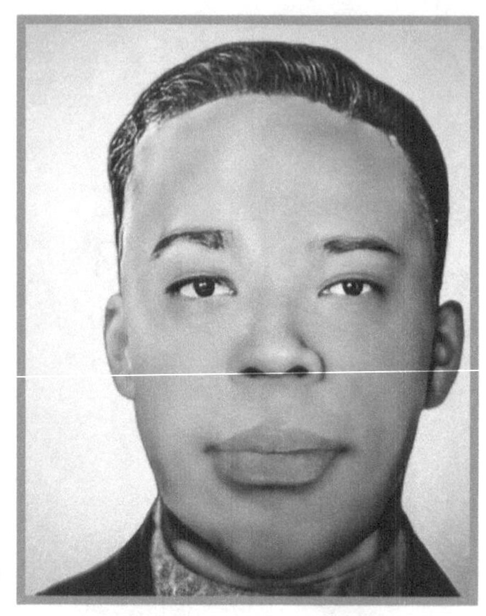

BERTRAND BLACKMORE

OLIVE BLACKMORE

MARGARET THERESA DEMPSTER CAESAR

THE BLACKMORE FAMILY: GORDON, LAWRENCE, MARIE, PATRICIA AND CEDRIC (TOP LEFT TO RIGHT). CLAIRE, OLIVE, MERVIN AND MONTY (BOTTOM LEFT TO RIGHT)

LAWRENCE BLACKMORE

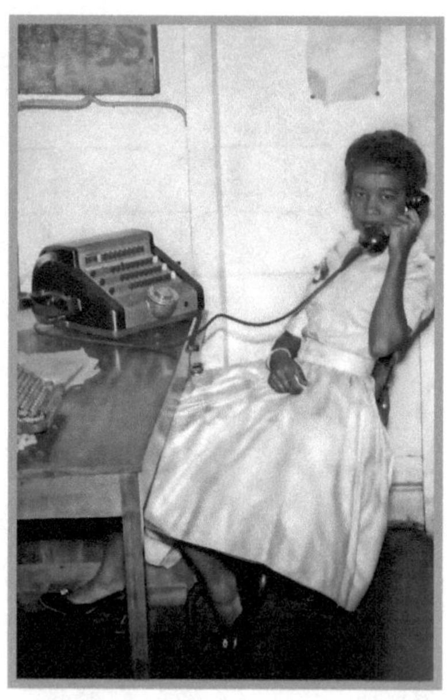

PATRICIA BLACKMORE AT WORK AT GUYANA GEOLOGICAL SURVEY

LEMUEL "PAPA" ANTHONY WALKING PATRICIA BLACKMORE UP THE AISLE AT THE CATHEDRAL OF THE IMMACULATE CONCEPTION IN A WEDDING DRESS DESIGNED AND MADE BY OLIVE BLACKMORE

PATRICIA BLACKMORE IN A WEDDING DRESS TRAIN DESIGNED AND MADE BY OLIVE BLACKMORE

PATRICIA'S WEDDING: OLIVE BLACKMORE, CLAIRE BLACKMORE, FRANCIS QUAMINA FARRIER, PATRICIA BLACKMORE FARRIER, MARIE BLACKMORE SMITH, GORDON BLACKMORE AND CEDRIC BLACKMORE (LEFT TO RIGHT)

WEDDING CAKE MADE BY OLIVE BLACKMORE AND DECORATED BY MRS. DEVONISH

OLIVE WITH HER EXTENDED FAMILY AND FRIENDS

CEDRIC AND CLAUDETTE BLACKMORE'S WEDDING

MONTY BLACKMORE WITH HIS BAND, THE JETS

CLAIRE BLACKMORE ON HER WEDDING DAY SURROUNDED BY HER NIECES NICOLA, MICHELLE (TOP), ABINA (BOTTOM), VENITA AND ARLENE (LEFT TO RIGHT)

OLIVE, WITH HER GRANDCHILDREN MICHELLE, NICOLA, VENITA AND ARLENE (LEFT TO RIGHT)

NICOLA, ABINA, ARLENE, VENITA AND MICHELLE (LEFT TO RIGHT)

VENITA, NICOLA, ARLENE AND MICHELLE (LEFT TO RIGHT) PERFORMING AT THE NATIONAL CULTURAL CENTER

OLIVE AND HER GRANDCHILDREN AT THE AIRPORT. NICOLA, MICHELLE, A FAMILY FRIEND (TOP), JERMAINE (BOTTOM), OLIVE (TOP), ABINA (BOTTOM), VENITA AND ARLENE (LEFT TO RIGHT)

ARLENE FARRIER AND VENITA FARRIER

JERMAINE MURRAY AND LISA MURRAY

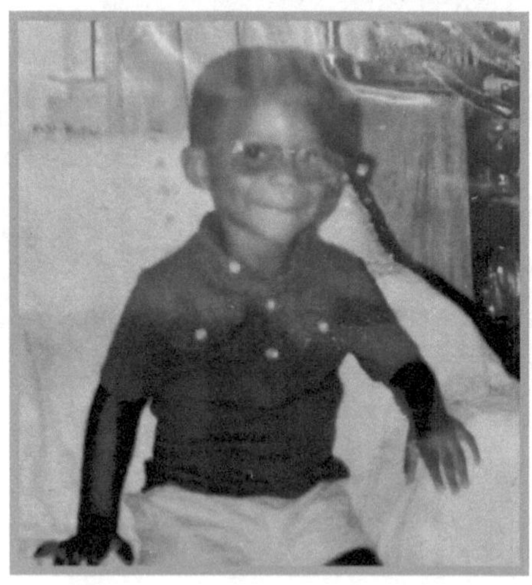

KEVIN BLACKMORE

ABINA BLACKMORE AND CEDRIC BLACKMORE, JR.

MERVIN BLACKMORE, JR.

NICOLAS BLACKMORE, LAWRENCE BLACKMORE AND LAUREL BLACKMORE

CHERYL BLACKMORE AND RAWLE BLACKMORE

OLIVE BLACKMORE, WITH HER SIBLINGS ERIC AND OLGA JOSEPH

PATRICIA AND OLIVE OUTSIDE THE MUSEUM OF NATURAL HISTORY IN NEW YORK

VENITA AND OLIVE ON THE STATUE OF LIBERTY

OLIVE ON THE STATUE OF LIBERTY WITH THE TWIN TOWERS IN THE BACKGROUND

PATRICIA, ARLENE AND OLIVE VISITING VENITA IN NEW YORK

ARLENE'S GRADUATION IN WASHINGTON D.C.: PATRICIA, FRANCIS, ARLENE, VENITA AND OLIVE (LEFT TO RIGHT)

OLIVE BLACKMORE OUTSIDE THE WHITE HOUSE IN WASHINGTON D.C.

OLIVE AND HER DAUGHTERS: MARIE, OLIVE, CLAIRE AND PATRICIA (LEFT TO RIGHT)

GORDON BLACKMORE AND OLIVE AT A FAMILY EVENT

GORDON, MARIE, PATRICIA AND CLAIR IN NEW YORK (LEFT TO RIGHT)

LAWRENCE, GORDON AND MONTY IN NEW YORK (LEFT TO RIGHT)

Olive with her sons Gordon and Lawrence on her birthday

The Blackmore brothers: Lawrence, Cedric, Monty, Mervin and Gordon (left to right)

Olive on her way to afternoon tea

OLIVE RELAXING AT HOME

OLIVE WITH HER HALF-SISTER EUNICE JOSEPH

OLIVE WITH HER GRANDSON, JERMAINE MURRAY

OLIVE DANCING WITH CEDRIC AT HER 100TH BIRTHDAY PARTY

OLIVE SITTING BY HER FAVORITE WINDOW AT HOME

OLIVE AND MERVIN

OLIVE AND MERVIN

OLIVE STILL CHEERFUL AFTER LOSING HER SIGHT

OLIVE WITH PRESIDENT DAVID GRANGER

OLIVE DANCING AT A FAMILY GATHERING

OLIVE AT 98 YEARS HAVING LUNCH AT CARA LODGE RESTAURANT

PATRICIA AND OLIVE

www.ingramcontent.com/pod-product-compliance
Lightning Source LLC
Chambersburg PA
CBHW051437140726
47987CB00006B/2423